J.O.Y.

Just Observe Yourself™

Mindfulness Meditation Journal
Ollie G. Goodlow, M.D., L.Ac

To Michele,
Wishing you a healthy happy & joyous life.
Ollie Goodlow

©2012 Ollie G. Goodlow, M.D., L.Ac

All rights reserved. No part of this publication may be reproduced, distributed, stored in a retrieval system, or transmitted in any form or by any means, including photocopying, recording or electronic methods or otherwise, without written permission by the author. For permission request email author at info@Drolliegoodlow.com.

LCCN 2011916564

Contents

Introduction..7

Getting Started..9

Mind, Body, Soul, and Reflection......................11

Day One...14

Reflections...74

About the Author......................................97

Acknowledgments.......................................99

References...100

This book is dedicated to my grandchildren:
Jacob, Jason, and Jordan.

Introduction

J.O.Y. JUST OBSERVE YOURSELF™ is a mindfulness meditation journal designed to support you while you discover how your thoughts create your life. Mindfulness teaches you to become aware of your thoughts, physical sensations, and emotions moment to moment without judgment. The practice leads to a deep awareness of yourself and your surroundings. This thirty-day journal encourages you to explore what's on your mind, check in with your body, and listen to your soul.

Are you living in the moment?

Many people are preoccupied with the past and worry about the future to such an extent that they miss the gift of the present moment. As spiritualist, Eckhart Tolle, said, "nothing happens outside the now." You now have the opportunity to learn to live in the moment, creating joy in your daily life. Mindfulness Meditation has been clinically proven to decrease stress and improve mood, memory and physical well being.

Your thoughts are like threads that come together to create a web. Your web is woven according to your own individual thoughts, beliefs, and experiences. Many people think the same thoughts without knowing, creating the same drama in their lives. This thirty-day journal urges you to see yourself on a deeper level .You now have an opportunity to discover just what is on your mind and what you are creating.

You can start right now; you don't need to purchase equipment or go to a special place. All you need is time and commitment to just observe yourself.

Getting Started

The program requires time and commitment to just observe yourself. There are two types of mindfulness meditation practices: formal and informal.

Formal practice begins with reading the inspirational quote. This gives you a positive mind-set before you start.

- You may sit in a chair or on the floor. If, seated in a chair, sit with a straight back, chin in and head balance. Place your feet flat on the floor uncrossed with hands on your lap palms up. Sit in a relax position not stiff or rigid, but comfortable and erect.

- Take three deep breaths, and then relax into your normal rhythm of breathing.

- Close your eyes or keep them open—whatever feels comfortable for you.

- Sit for a moment and just observe yourself. Feel the surface that is supporting you.

- Bring your attention to your breath at the level of your nostrils or lower abdomen. Choose a place where you feel the sensation the most. Just observe yourself with each inhalation and exhalation.

- When thoughts come up, notice what's on your mind, and then gently release the thought. The mind's job is to think thoughts. You are not trying to stop the thoughts. Just observe yourself without judging yourself. Gently bring your attention back to your breath.

- After sitting for twenty minutes, complete one Mind, Body, and Soul exercise daily, using the journal pages.

Informal practice begins with taking time to connect with your breath to anchor you to the moment throughout the day.

- You may want to set different signals to remind you to connect with your breath.

- For example, when the phone rings, entering or leaving a room, washing your hands and when you feel stressed. Just observe yourself without judging yourself. Observe thoughts, body sensations and emotions. Your breath is with you wherever you go; just take time to connect.

- Repeat this process each day for the next thirty days.

- At the end of thirty days, complete the Reflection pages.

Each thought is a gift that allows you to open the door into your inner world. What are you creating? Buddha said, "What we think we become." Now, with awareness of your thoughts, you have an opportunity to create a joyful life.

Mind, Body, Soul, and Reflection

Mind

- Write what thoughts are on your mind.

Body

- Check in with your body.
- Is a particular body part asking for your attention?
- Bring your awareness to that body part. Do you have tension or pain? Ask your body part what it is trying to tell you. Be still, and then write the first thing that comes to your mind.

Soul

- Ask for guidance.
- Listen and just be.
- Without censoring, write what comes to mind and how you are feeling. If you feel you are not hearing or feeling anything, don't worry. When the time is right, you will hear and know your own truth.
- Be grateful for your existence and for the time spent with others here and now.
- Write three things for which you are grateful.

- Bring your awareness to your chest and feel the sensation of joy and peace within.

Repeat the Mind, Body, and Soul exercise for each of the thirty days.

Reflection

- Are there recurring themes in your journal entries?
- Do you have discomfort in the same areas consistently, or changing areas?
- Were your thoughts negative or positive?
- Did find your thoughts to be true?
- What did you discover about yourself?
- Can you practice being in the moment more often?

Day One

We are shaped by our thoughts; we become what we think. When the mind is pure, joy follows like a shadow that never leaves. ~Buddha

Mind - The thoughts on my mind are:

Body - My Body is telling me:

Soul - Ask for guidance: _____

_____
_____
_____
_____
_____
_____
_____

Write three things you are grateful for: _____

_____
_____
_____
_____
_____
_____
_____
_____
_____
_____
_____
_____

Day Two

Everyone has been made for some particular work, and the desire for that work has been put in every heart. ~ Rumi

Mind - The thoughts on my mind are: _____

Body - My Body is telling me: _____

Soul - Ask for guidance: _____

_____
_____
_____
_____
_____
_____
_____
_____

Write three things you are grateful for: _____

_____
_____
_____
_____
_____
_____
_____
_____
_____
_____
_____
_____
_____
_____
_____
_____

Day Three

Every human being is the author of his own health or disease. ~ Buddha

Mind - The thoughts on my mind are:_____

_____
_____
_____
_____
_____
_____
_____
_____
_____

Body - My Body is telling me:_____

_____
_____
_____
_____
_____
_____
_____
_____
_____
_____
_____

Soul - Ask for guidance: _____

Write three things you are grateful for: _____

Day Four

Let the beauty of what you love be what you do. ~ Rumi

Mind - The thoughts on my mind are: _____

Body - My Body is telling me: _____

Soul - Ask for guidance: _____

_____
_____
_____
_____
_____
_____
_____
_____
_____

Write three things you are grateful for: _____

_____
_____
_____
_____
_____
_____
_____
_____
_____
_____
_____
_____
_____
_____
_____
_____

Day Five

It is better to travel well than to arrive. ~ Buddha

Mind - The thoughts on my mind are:

Body - My Body is telling me:

Soul - Ask for guidance: _____

Write three things you are grateful for: _____

Day Six

This world offers no beauty like the beauty inside. Oh my heart! Unpack your journey's luggage here. . ~ Rumi

Mind - The thoughts on my mind are:

Body - My Body is telling me:

Soul - Ask for guidance: _____

_____
_____
_____
_____
_____
_____
_____
_____
_____

Write three things you are grateful for: _____

_____
_____
_____
_____
_____
_____
_____
_____
_____
_____
_____
_____
_____
_____
_____

Day Seven

Peace comes from within. Do not seek it without. ~ Buddha

Mind - The thoughts on my mind are:_____

_____
_____
_____
_____
_____
_____
_____
_____
_____
_____

Body - My Body is telling me:_____

_____
_____
_____
_____
_____
_____
_____
_____
_____
_____

Soul - Ask for guidance: _____

Write three things you are grateful for: _____

Day Eight

Observe the wonders as they occur around you. Don't claim them. Feel the artistry moving through and be silent. ~ Rumi

Mind - The thoughts on my mind are:

Body - My Body is telling me:

Soul - Ask for guidance: _____

Write three things you are grateful for: _____

Day Nine

You yourself, as much as anybody in the entire universe, deserve your love and affection. ~ Buddha

Mind - The thoughts on my mind are:

Body - My Body is telling me:

Soul - Ask for guidance: _____

Write three things you are grateful for: _____

Day Ten

The minute I heard my first love story, I started looking for you, not knowing how blind that was. Lovers don't finally meet somewhere. They're in each other all along. ~ Rumi

Mind - The thoughts on my mind are: _____

Body - My Body is telling me: _____

Soul - Ask for guidance: _____

_____
_____
_____
_____
_____
_____
_____
_____

Write three things you are grateful for: _____

_____
_____
_____
_____
_____
_____
_____
_____
_____
_____
_____
_____
_____
_____
_____

Day Eleven

To understand everything is to forgive everything. ~ Buddha

Mind - The thoughts on my mind are: _____

_____
_____
_____
_____
_____
_____
_____
_____
_____

Body - My Body is telling me: _____

_____
_____
_____
_____
_____
_____
_____
_____
_____
_____
_____

Soul - Ask for guidance: _____

Write three things you are grateful for: _____

Day Twelve

When you do things from the soul, you feel a river moving in you, a joy. ~ Rumi

Mind - The thoughts on my mind are:
_____
_____
_____
_____
_____
_____
_____
_____
_____
_____
_____
_____

Body - My Body is telling me:
_____
_____
_____
_____
_____
_____
_____
_____
_____
_____
_____
_____
_____

Soul - Ask for guidance: _____

_____
_____
_____
_____
_____
_____
_____
_____

Write three things you are grateful for: _____

_____
_____
_____
_____
_____
_____
_____
_____
_____
_____
_____
_____
_____
_____
_____

Day Thirteen

**The mind is everything. What you think you become.
~ Buddha**

Mind - The thoughts on my mind are:_____

_____
_____
_____
_____
_____
_____
_____
_____
_____
_____

Body - My Body is telling me:_____

_____
_____
_____
_____
_____
_____
_____
_____
_____
_____
_____
_____
_____

Soul - Ask for guidance: _____

_____
_____
_____
_____
_____
_____
_____
_____
_____
_____

Write three things you are grateful for: _____

_____
_____
_____
_____
_____
_____
_____
_____
_____
_____
_____
_____
_____
_____
_____
_____
_____
_____

Day Fourteen

Stop the words now. Open the window in the center of your chest and let the spirit fly in and out. ~ Rumi

Mind - The thoughts on my mind are: _____

_____
_____
_____
_____
_____
_____
_____
_____
_____

Body - My Body is telling me: _____

_____
_____
_____
_____
_____
_____
_____
_____
_____
_____
_____

Soul - Ask for guidance: _____

_____
_____
_____
_____
_____
_____
_____
_____

Write three things you are grateful for: _____

_____
_____
_____
_____
_____
_____
_____
_____
_____
_____
_____
_____
_____
_____
_____
_____

Day Fifteen

Do not dwell in the past, do not dream of the future, concentrate the mind on the present moment. ~ Buddha

Mind - The thoughts on my mind are:_____

_____
_____
_____
_____
_____
_____
_____
_____
_____
_____

Body - My Body is telling me:_____

_____
_____
_____
_____
_____
_____
_____
_____
_____
_____
_____
_____
_____

Soul - Ask for guidance: _____

_____
_____
_____
_____
_____
_____
_____
_____

Write three things you are grateful for: _____

_____
_____
_____
_____
_____
_____
_____
_____
_____
_____
_____
_____
_____
_____
_____

Day Sixteen

I want to sing like the birds sing, not worrying about who hears or what they think. ~ Rumi

Mind - The thoughts on my mind are: _____

Body - My Body is telling me: _____

Soul - Ask for guidance: _____

_____
_____
_____
_____
_____
_____
_____
_____

Write three things you are grateful for: _____

_____
_____
_____
_____
_____
_____
_____
_____
_____
_____
_____
_____
_____
_____
_____

Day Seventeen

Thousands of candles can be lit from a single candle, and the life of the candle will not be shortened. Happiness never decreases by being shared. ~ Buddha

Mind - The thoughts on my mind are:

Body - My Body is telling me:

Soul - Ask for guidance: _____

Write three things you are grateful for: _____

Day Eighteen

People of the world don't look at themselves and so they blame one another. ~ Rumi

Mind - The thoughts on my mind are:

Body - My Body is telling me:

Soul - Ask for guidance: _____

_____
_____
_____
_____
_____
_____
_____
_____

Write three things you are grateful for: _____

_____
_____
_____
_____
_____
_____
_____
_____
_____
_____
_____
_____
_____
_____
_____

Day Nineteen

An idea that is developed and put into action is more important than an idea that exists only as an idea. ~ Buddha

Mind - The thoughts on my mind are:_____

_____
_____
_____
_____
_____
_____
_____
_____
_____
_____
_____

Body - My Body is telling me:_____

_____
_____
_____
_____
_____
_____
_____
_____
_____
_____
_____
_____

Soul - Ask for guidance: _____

Write three things you are grateful for: _____

Day Twenty

Love said to me, there is nothing that is not me. Be silent. ~ Rumi

Mind - The thoughts on my mind are:

Body - My Body is telling me:

Soul - Ask for guidance: _____

Write three things you are grateful for: _____

Day Twenty-one

Be the witness of your thoughts - Buddha

Mind - The thoughts on my mind are: _____

Body - My Body is telling me: _____

Soul - Ask for guidance: _____

Write three things you are grateful for: _____

Day Twenty-two

Let yourself be silently drawn by the stronger pull of what you really love. ~ Rumi

Mind - The thoughts on my mind are:

Body - My Body is telling me:

Soul - Ask for guidance: _____

_____
_____
_____
_____
_____
_____
_____
_____
_____

Write three things you are grateful for: _____

_____
_____
_____
_____
_____
_____
_____
_____
_____
_____
_____
_____
_____
_____
_____
_____

Day Twenty-three

To keep the body in good health is a duty...otherwise we shall not be able to keep our mind strong and clear. ~ Buddha

Mind - The thoughts on my mind are:

Body - My Body is telling me:

Soul - Ask for guidance: _____

_____
_____
_____
_____
_____
_____
_____

Write three things you are grateful for: _____

_____
_____
_____
_____
_____
_____
_____
_____
_____
_____
_____
_____
_____

Day Twenty-four

Let go of your mind and then be mindful. Close your ears and listen!. ~ Rumi

Mind - The thoughts on my mind are: _____

_____
_____
_____
_____
_____
_____
_____
_____
_____

Body - My Body is telling me: _____

_____
_____
_____
_____
_____
_____
_____
_____
_____
_____
_____
_____
_____

Soul - Ask for guidance: _____

Write three things you are grateful for: _____

Day Twenty-five

We are what we think. All that we are arrives with our thought. With thought we make the world. ~ Buddha

Mind - The thoughts on my mind are:

Body - My Body is telling me:

Soul - Ask for guidance: _____

_____
_____
_____
_____
_____
_____
_____
_____

Write three things you are grateful for: _____

_____
_____
_____
_____
_____
_____
_____
_____
_____
_____
_____
_____
_____
_____
_____
_____

Day Twenty-six

Here is a letter to everyone. You open it. It says, "Live."
~ Rumi

Mind - The thoughts on my mind are: _____

_____
_____
_____
_____
_____
_____
_____
_____
_____

Body - My Body is telling me: _____

_____
_____
_____
_____
_____
_____
_____
_____
_____
_____
_____
_____

Soul - Ask for guidance: _____

_____
_____
_____
_____
_____
_____
_____
_____

Write three things you are grateful for: _____

_____
_____
_____
_____
_____
_____
_____
_____
_____
_____
_____
_____
_____
_____

Day Twenty-seven

Health is the greatest gift, contentment the greatest wealth, faithfulness the best relationship. ~ Buddha

Mind - The thoughts on my mind are:

_____
_____
_____
_____
_____
_____
_____
_____
_____
_____

Body - My Body is telling me:

_____
_____
_____
_____
_____
_____
_____
_____
_____
_____
_____
_____

Soul - Ask for guidance: _____

Write three things you are grateful for: _____

Day Twenty-eight

Be empty of worrying. Think of who created thought.
~ Rumi

Mind - The thoughts on my mind are:

Body - My Body is telling me:

Soul - Ask for guidance: _____

_____
_____
_____
_____
_____
_____
_____
_____

Write three things you are grateful for: _____

_____
_____
_____
_____
_____
_____
_____
_____
_____
_____
_____
_____
_____
_____

Day Twenty-nine

Better than a thousand hollow words, is one word that brings peace. ~ Buddha

Mind - The thoughts on my mind are:

Body - My Body is telling me:

Soul - Ask for guidance: _____

_____
_____
_____
_____
_____
_____
_____
_____
_____

Write three things you are grateful for: _____

_____
_____
_____
_____
_____
_____
_____
_____
_____
_____
_____
_____
_____
_____
_____
_____

Day Thirty

Patience in the key to joy. ~ Rumi

Mind - The thoughts on my mind are:

Body - My Body is telling me:

Soul - Ask for guidance: _____

_____
_____
_____
_____
_____
_____
_____
_____
_____

Write three things you are grateful for: _____

_____
_____
_____
_____
_____
_____
_____
_____
_____
_____
_____
_____
_____
_____
_____
_____

Reflection

1. Are there recurring themes in your journal entries?

Reflection

2. Do you have discomfort in the same areas consistently or changing areas?

Reflection

3. Were your thoughts negative or positive?

Reflection

4. Did you find your thoughts to be true?

Reflection

5. What did you discover about yourself?

Reflection

6. Can you practice being in the moment more often?

Notes

Notes

Notes

Notes

Notes

Notes

Notes

Notes

Notes

Notes

Notes

Notes

Notes

Notes

Notes

Notes

Notes

About the Author

Ollie G. Goodlow, M.D., L.Ac, is a practicing diagnostic radiologist in the Washington, D.C., metropolitan area. Dr. Goodlow has been teaching Mind Body Wellness for twenty years, and is the founder and executive director of Creative Transformation Wellness Programs.

Dr. Goodlow trained with Jon Kabat-Zin, the developer of the nationally recognized Mindfulness-Based Stress Reduction program (MBSR) in tandem with the University of Massachusetts. She pioneered the first pilot Mindfulness Meditation program in Landover, Maryland, at one of the largest health maintenance organizations in the country, Kaiser Permanente. In an effort to expand her understanding of Eastern medicine, Dr. Goodlow became a licensed acupuncturist with training at the UCLA School of Medicine.

Dr. Goodlow is currently teaching her wellness program at a drug rehabilitation program in Washington, D.C. Her motto is *Meditate Before You Medicate*™.

Keep up with Dr. Goodlow by visiting her website, www.drolliegoodlow.com. Look for her soon-to-be-published J.O.Y. Just Observe Yourself Meditation Workbook and meditation CD.

Acknowledgements

I gratefully acknowledge those who labor before me, who have passed down through the ages these ancient teachings of Buddha and Rumi.

My greatest thanks go to Rudy Coleman, my mentor, who encouraged me to write this book. His guidance and support made this book a reality.

With love and gratitude I want to thank my family and friends for their support throughout the journey.

References

Byrom, T. 1991. *Dhammapada The Sayings of the Buddha*. Boston: Shambhala

Hadland Davis, F. 1907. *The Persian Mystics Jalalud-Din Rumi*. London

Kabat-Zinn, J. 1990. *Full Catastrophic Living: Using the Wisdom of Your Body Mind to Face Stress, Pain,and Illness*. New York: Delacourt.

Kabat-Zinn, J. 1994. *Wherever You Go There You Are: Mindfulness Meditation in Everyday Life*. New York: Hyperion

Tolle, E. 1999. *The Power of Now*. Novato, CA: New World Publishing.

Tolle, E. 2001. *Practicing the Power of Now*. Novato, CA: New World Publishing.

Made in the USA
Charleston, SC
11 August 2012